My Psychic

MY PSYCHIC POEMS James Kimbrell

[handwritten signature: James Kimbrell]

[handwritten inscription:]

For Morri,

With gratitude for your friendship & admiration & love for your poems. Good to see you again!

Cheers,
Tallahassee Oct 2006 Jim

Sarabande Books
LOUISVILLE, KENTUCKY

Managing Editor
Sarabande Books, Inc.
2234 Dundee Road, Suite 200
Louisville, KY 40205

Library of Congress Cataloging-in-Publication Data

Kimbrell, James, 1967–
      My psychic : poems / by James Kimbrell.— 1st ed.
          p.   cm.
      ISBN-13: 978-1-932511-25-3 (pbk. : acid-free paper)
    I. Title.

    PS3561.I41677M92 2006
    811'.54—dc22   2005028134

ISBN-13: 978-1-932-51125-3; ISBN-10: 1-932511-25-3

Cover image: Illustrations from the Rider-Waite Tarot Deck® reproduced by permission of U.S. Games Systems, Inc., Stamford, CT 06902 USA. Copyright © 1971 by U.S. Games Systems, Inc. Further reproduction prohibited. The Rider-Waite Tarot Deck® is a registered trademark of U.S. Games Systems, Inc.

Cover and text design by Charles Casey Martin
Printed in Canada
This book is printed on acid-free paper.
Sarabande Books is a nonprofit literary organization.

THE KENTUCKY ARTS COUNCIL

The Kentucky Arts Council, a state agency in the Commerce Cabinet, provides operational support funding for Sarabande Books with state tax dollars and federal funding from the National Endowment for the Arts, which believes that a great nation deserves great art.

This book is for my mother
Margaret Lack Kimbrell
1942–2000

Contents

Acknowledgments   ix

I.

My Psychic   3

Four Tangerines   6

But Thou Has Played the Harlot with Many Lovers;
   Yet Return Again to Me   8

Ode   11

Drought Music   12

Blackberry Winter   14

On Teaching   16

Sometimes a Cloud Looks Like a Getaway Car Again   19

Don't Drive to the Beach Alone   21

II. Love Had a Thousand Shapes

   i. Love had a thousand shapes...   25

   ii. When I was a child my mother would stare...   26

   iii. Soon as the last bag of black beans...   27

   iv. We broached it speculatively, the "afterlife"...   29

   v. My mother calls to talk about what a terrible...   31

   vi. I kiss her on the forehead, put my arm around her... 32

   vii. My mother swatting a mosquito off my shoulder...   33

   viii. When I return from the hospital...   34

   ix. Far to the left of the placard that read ETERNAL... 35

   x. My mother and her friends by the apartment pool...   36

xi. My sense that things were poorly rehearsed... 37

xii. Everywhere I went my mother went with me... 38

xiii. After the dream I pull the ottoman... 39

xiv. More than twice the amount that her check could pay... 40

xv. There is the shape of sound: someone passing... 41

III.

Depression in May 45

Praise for the Ford LTD 46

Wings 49

Bahia Grass 51

To Keats in October 53

The Gulf 54

Up Late, Reading Whitman 56

The Author 63

Acknowledgments

I would like to thank the editors of the following magazines in which several of the poems in this collection first appeared, some in slightly different versions.

Black Warrior Review: "Bahia Grass," "Drought Music," "Wings"

Cairn: "But Thou Hast Played the Harlot with Many Lovers; Yet Return Again to Me," "Sometimes a Cloud Looks Like a Getaway Car Again," "Don't Drive to the Beach Alone"

Cincinnati Review: "Praise for the Ford LTD," "We broached it speculatively, the 'afterlife'...," "I kiss her on the forehead, put my arm around her...," "More than twice the amount that her check could pay"

Chelsea: "Ode," as "Lover's Moon"

Gulf Coast: "Four Tangerines"

The Kenyon Review: "Up Late, Reading Whitman"

Meridian: "Far to the left of the placard that read ETERNAL URNS," "My mother swatting a mosquito off my shoulder," "Love had a thousand shapes..."

Miller's Pond: "My sense that things were poorly rehearsed..."

Poetry: "Blackberry Winter," "To Keats in October," "My Psychic"

64: "Soon as the last bag of black beans," as "The Currency"

Washington Square: "Depression in May"

Several of these poems have also appeared in *Poetry 30: Thirty-something Thirtysomething American Poets,* (eds. Daniel Crocker and

Gerry LaFemina, Mammoth Books, 2005) and in *Legitimate Dangers: American Poets of the New Century* (eds. Michael Dumanis and Cate Marvin, Sarabande Books, 2006).

My sincere gratitude to the Mrs. Giles Whiting Foundation, the Sewanee Writer's Conference, the Florida Arts Council, and the National Endowment for the Arts for their generous support. Thanks also to the Florida State University for funding and release time that was of tremendous assistance in the completion of this book.

Epigraph translated by Frank O. Copley.

For mark those bodies which, though known to be
In this our world, are yet invisible...
                                    —Lucretius, *De Rerum Natura*

My Psychic

I

My Psychic

has a giant hand
        diagrammed in front of her place
on West Tennessee.
        It towers above a kudzu hill as if
    to offer a cosmic *How!*
                as in *Hello!* from a long
way off, as in how

she already knows
        the sundry screwed up ways a day
can go days before
        I park my wreck on the hill again beside
    her white Mercedes. O
            little slice of Lebanon!
O cedar scented

cards fanned like feathers
        of a Byzantine peacock! Tell
me again how I
        might have been a fine lawyer, that I'll raise
    four kids in Tallahassee, how
            I married—it's true—on
my lunch break—*Yez*

she took you to lunch

       okay a zeven year lunch ha ha!

Incense. Mini-shrine.

       A wagon train of chihuahuas snoozing by

    her slippers. *You have anxious*

       about a future . . . I do. But

lately I've grown cold,

unconsoled by her

       extrasensory view. I think

—no need to speak—across

       the black tabletop, I don't want to know

    if I'll find a bright city,

       a room by the river, a love

I will recognize

by her dragonfly

       tattoo. O narrative of ether!

O non-refundable

       life facts! say that what happens may not matter,

    or that it matters as any

       story does when two fresh lovers

embrace the old pact

(her bra on the chair,

       his socks in the kitchen) that says

their love is level,

       unfabled, new. Level with me, tell me why

    the dogs on the floor, little

                   moon-fed hounds of Delphi, seem
so over it, so

done with the fleas of
              destiny. Maybe that's the right
attitude, no need
              to ask why I'm here on a perfectly blue
       Friday, content with
                    what the thin air, what the dust
motes in the light say

near the high window. I
              should've learned that music long ago—
O soundless number!
              O jukebox of being that the dogs dream to! No
       faux crystal ball, no tea leaves
                    or terrace in the nether
reaches of my palm

will make her answers
              less like hocus-pocus in a purchased dark.
It's time to pay, to drive away
              from telepathic altitudes, to say adieu
       to why love ends. How
              a heart opens again. Why
anything is true.

Four Tangerines

1   1985: In my dream an elderly man climbs through the window wearing only boxers and a threadbare tank top. His hair is dripping and it appears as though he swam a great distance. He opens the door to my closet. "Mine!" he says, touching the white shirt. The gabardine suit. The green wool sweater with leather patches on the elbows and shoulders. You can have them back, I say. I can give you some money. "Do you have a tangerine?" he asks. "All I want is a tangerine."

2   Williams? Miller? You are born and are given a name. You are clothed. One day you die in the nursing home where my mother works. I walk through the tomato garden. I let the beaded water shine your shoes. Your shirt is baggy and bright and spotless in the sun. When I wear your clothes, is there something of the living in you? Of the dead in me? Vast cities between cloth and skin? I'm with my friends, standing around in the parking lot, talking before school.

3   When given the assignment to write a poem in the style of your favorite poet, I choose Edgar Allan Poe. The best poems will be posted on the east wall of the classroom just above the desk of the lovely woman child, Annabel Lee, a.k.a. Trish. Sunday night, I stare at Poe's picture in our anthology as if it were a mirror. My poem is entitled, "The Consequences of Life" and is all about death, but with a social message: I think Trish should accompany me to the senior

dance. I think that Poe would not disagree with the exact fit of a dead man's clothes.

4   I picture you watching me as if I were a small man in a small town inside a snow-globe. You see the shoes you checked the mail in. The pants you jitterbugged in, one December, alive, beside yourself. You are so far away from me, there is no way to thank you. You do not know my name. I never hear yours. I think of you as "Addlestien, the Memphis Taylor," which is stitched to the inside pocket of your black coat. The same coat that I wear, cutting a sharp figure, or so I imagine, walking home past the cornfield with its poorly attired scarecrow.

But Thou Hast Played the Harlot with Many Lovers; Yet Return Again to Me

1.

Forgive me: the desire to walk over the dunes beyond the sea oats and
     into the gulf
until the saltwater baptizes my cochlea

is a desire for Ferris wheels...

Twelve years old. My best friend's mother has a fish tank in her bedroom
     in which sits
a miniature Ferris wheel spun by bubbles,

and as I lie there smelling her pillow

(it is my practice to enter their house when no one is home)

I think how wonderful if she and I could sit next to each other in the
     round tower
of this ocean kingdom, my hand in her hair, my mouth on her breast,
     and if her
Sunday hat flies off

I will leap from my seat and dog-paddle through the air...

2.

From my window across the street, I watch her lovers come and go.

Farewell from behind a screen door.

Farewell of thigh visible through the split in her housecoat.

I particularly dislike the preacher with the bible verse bumper sticker
on his Mercury. He parks in front of her house each week, which
is the least he can do (her other child is his scandal).

I dream her in need of rescue. I dream that when the preacher is done
    that I, too,

                might

(we lie down in our shame, and our confusion covereth us).

3.

Cotton candy.
Apricots.
State fair taffy pulled like a giant sugar muscle between two mechanical
    rolling pins.
Tea olive in early autumn.
Cane juice on a knife blade.
Hairspray.
Pears roasted in their skins.
Faint trace of cat piss.

Cut grass behind a cigar factory.

Cedars of Lebanon.

Pines of Pascagoula.

Gardenia.

Honeysuckle.

Frangipani.

Of these aromas and more is my beloved's pillow made.

4.

I hear their car pulling into the drive, the station wagon belching blue smoke. In seconds I am standing beneath the plywood backboard, spinning the basketball on my fingertip. Her son comes whistling out the back door. He doesn't so much as look at me funny.

I never enter that house again. Mine is the sort of exhilaration mixed with guilt that will leave Vaseline stains on my bible pages.

Forgive me: when the smell of a hundred suppers drifts out across the ligustrum, and my beloved leans from the window and calls her son in, her hair is not as a flock of goats that appear from Gilead,

but I can not look away from her.

My dove, I think, my undefiled, my head is filled with dew.

Ode

Horace to Lydia, 23 B.C.: "Now the only rocks that tap your window are thrown by the wheels of chariots burning to get away from you. I hate to say it, Lydia, but the sweet sound of your door swinging on its oiled hinges, that constant creak that once would have laid the sweetest nightingale to shame, is no song now. There's hardly a note save for the bleating of dust in the jambs. You'd play hell hearing another boy in the night's honeyed middle nudging you, pining, 'Hey Lyd, wake up, I scored some killer goat's milk!' To see you these days, walking with the unmistakable saddle-like sway of the hopelessly wallowed out, is to see the moon herself, that old love-starved queen. How quickly she turns from white to green upon witnessing her own best light shining now on the leaves of the myrtle, on the thighs and sleek shoulders of lovers swimming in the knee-high grass." Or, in other words, "Open the Goddamn door, Lydia. I LOVE YOU!"

Drought Music

Now that the fly dozes on the swollen armadillo,
  and the clouds cruise like Winnabagos above
    the streams and green highways way north of here,
      now that tempers flare and doors slam and not
        speaking is agreed upon, what cooler, what speedier
          oblivion than this piped-in thunderhead that I
            direct from chinaberry to flowerbed, a ritual drench
              worlds away from our last squabble. Something

about who took the message, who lost the keys,
  who left the laundry door unlatched, something
    that ended with giving up, with walking out
      about as far as the hose would stretch. I would go
        back in were it not for the smell of fig leaves
          doused with hose water, were it not for the twitch
            of the neighbor's fancy sprinkler pulsing trochees,
              then reversing into *forget...forget...* exactly

what I want to do, the whole who-said-what
  and what-was-meant forgotten between elephant ear
    and airplane plant. And what I wouldn't give
      to forget what we're finally fighting about—whether
        or not our love is worn out, finished with you
          banging the table and pushing back your chair,

finished with me stomping out here to wash
the dust from the shallow air, to compose my side

of the apology, which I suppose, like the rain,
is long past due. I know. I ought to cut this foolishness
off at the spigot. I ought to go back inside to you.
I will. I promise to. Soon as my shoes are soggy
and the brick walk to the mailbox is bordered
by a moat. Soon as water swells against the sun-warped
bluebells, the blackened ferns, the parched azaleas,
the many mini-deserts where the grass lost root.

Blackberry Winter

The birdbath water that cupped
the moon had bloomed to slush, acacia
and ivy bejeweled with ice, spring gone maniacally
astray when we stepped out, unbedded, in love
and in May, or at least in May, which seemed
enough, or had that day on the rural routes
where we wound up, windows

down, drinking hot beer
with descending cheers—*To both of you!*
To you! To us! Even after we'd stopped, picked
berries in ditches, then peed, then drove
away, we both knew what we were up to
with my date set, and you, uh, *practically*
engaged. And yet, with what

ease, what facility
did we slip into that body of facts
with two backs, a corpus ruminatum that we
perused separately the next thawed afternoon,
too flustered to phone, too embarrassed
to speak if we happened to see one
another paired with our

respective others across
the haze of some bar or cafe on an otherwise
unremarkable day. Nothing, so far, has frozen
this May. No love bewildered, none betrayed.
As for the trees—green notes of the air—
they hover with the moon in a skillet of water
past three a.m. when I

walk out to call the dog in.
What breeze there is does not sway
the branches, nor does time's wand wave or blend
any past lapse of common sense into
a clarified present tense: the clouds
push along at a summer's pace, the wisteria
is sprouting, climbing the fences,

the whole world smells
like fresh cut grass. And there it is, faith-
ful as ever, frozen in place: the memory
not of our ascending from a drunken rush,
an error of flesh out of season and bounds,
but nature's joke, Jack's revenge—fog
rising from our wordless mouths.

On Teaching

1.

It seems wrong to erase the last professor's
blackboard notes. Not unlucky, not sinful,
but an insult to the recent past which still
smells like linoleum, shampoo, and pencils.
I'd rather sit and watch the oversized clock,
each desk empty, each window the measure
of its own light. Soon the air will fill with
hands that flutter like the laurel in spring.
Branches and voices. The commerce of words.
Sophistry in the lyceum of daydream.

2.

When I was a child I'd point the boxed
record player out the bedroom window.
"Blueberry Hill" to the shed roof, to the
tiller shut down midrow. "Aint That a Shame"
to the night-folded leaves of the spangly
mimosa, to the bass-boat afloat in an ocean
of crickets and rotting pears. Time is
a canvas, says Thoreau. You must toss
the reigns on the horse's neck, says Emerson.
I'm in love again, says Fats Domino.

3.

IS LOVE FAIR?—my blackboard question
for the hour. *Who cares?* is what these two
might say, arriving as they do each day, hand
in hand, his shirt wrinkled as a bed sheet,
her's all midriff, hardly there. I want to say,
"Don't look so bored! High above you
is the 'chairness' of chair. And it's a classic!"
But they aren't bored. They're in love. Small
difference, but nonetheless. Their days still
passion-shocked, brimming, over-blessed . . .

4.

Some ultra potent styling gel, those last drops
of *le vin herbez* in Tristan's beard, and Iseult
can't keep her fool mouth from the full
course meal of him. No red hot iron or town
of lepers, no kingly sword or flour spread
on the boudoir floor can keep these two
off each other. . . . The moral of the story?
Don't come knocking when the white sail
is rocking. Don't deny the heart its real
illusions. Don't fight monsters. Avoid golden hair.

5.

I can't convince them that class is short,
that loves are numbered, that beauty resides
in dishabille. Leaves in the windowsill.
Light that seeps through the wall where the painted

lumber rots. Uncertainty on a stairwell
two aging lovers stand atop. The mop of hair
that's yours, O youth, once was theirs.
'Twas the dream enchanted me, you might
say from a far address, and descend
into a mortal body. Its brevity. Its loveliness.

6.
"Are we going to be tested on this?" one
student asks. Then another: "Why do all
the love stories end in death?" Now that
their singles' cruise is a sinking ship, I wish
that I could take it back. "Forget that,"
I start, "the poet says 'death is the mother
of beauty,'" and sigh, assured they're not buying it.
Already, the room is a racket of books
slamming shut. Love, that quickest of powers,
bolts for the door at the end of the hour.

Sometimes a Cloud Looks Like a Getaway Car Again

As in Bonnie and Clyde pursued by a convoy of feds
on a corn-bordered road through nowhere, Missouri.
      My ex once said those smooching bandits bloomed
    into outlaws of heroic dimension
not by robbing banks, but by robbing banks together,
      by holding hands over the roof
    of their hijacked car for one more
          otherwise innocent picture.

     That seemed right that afternoon in the hammock
when she wore nothing but *The Lives and Times*
        of Bonnie and Clyde in her lap while I flapped
    like a landlocked bird trying to fan
the mosquitoes away. NO SHERIFF GREATER THAN LOVE
      is what she penned above
    her favorite picture in that book. And what
        did I say? It was one

    of those early days when the clouds might have been
a wedding procession, a carpet of white roses,
      a carriage pulled by snowy stallions
    on their connubial journey to the cotton palace. That's all
I remember. Now the sky is graced
      with a dingy rug, a bachelor's dull

kitchen curtain. Now I'm Clyde

                    in the Waco lockup, and when

        a cloud looks like a getaway car, I want to drive
that pillowy racer down my ex's street

              because my closest friend is still her absence
        and I thought they might like

to meet each other. But I stay put. I let the clouds

              pass over. As Clyde counted cash, I can count
        the lies I told. Her reciprocal

                    betrayals. Years from now

        she will seem a far-flung legend. I will remember
her with or without regret. A cloud

              will resemble her favorite summer dress.
        A cloud will appear to be the fat gardenia

that I cut from a stranger's yard

              on my way to her house, all hope
        and best shirt at sunset, willing

                    to steal anything for love.

Don't Drive to the Beach Alone

The gulls and ghost crabs are at war with each other. The blue mist of the vanishing point points only to itself. Don't stab the sand with the pole of your umbrella. The beach is not the moon. Gravity applies there. Sea horses don't wear saddles. Don't take your books and your blank sheet of paper. Don't begin that romantic conversation with yourself, *where light on the water outshines the past . . .*

Or better yet, drive fast, south toward the little town by the bay with the funeral home that doubles as a wedding chapel. Past the baroque long-beaked birds and the oyster house and the scent of pine needles sautéed in the sun.

But take your new love with you. Out there, everything will be better. Out there, you can start over. You can stay for two weeks and pretend your ship has capsized. You can make your own language together. Change your l's to r's and say "I ruv you ruvr." You can change the names of everything. You can walk out to the balcony and bring your love an apple, and say, "Fire truck, anyone?"

At midnight, the sand will glow beneath your feet with phosphorescent plankton. You will hold each other as gods do with stars warming your toes. You can have a costume party for two. You can go as lightning. Go as a volcano. Go as The Big Bang.

It will seem strange at first, this new happiness. You will be right to not trust it. You will wake alone beneath a stiff blanket in the cheap motel. From the shower you will hear the words: *I love you.* You will hear your voice echo this. You will rise and step toward the fluorescent mist. You will not be able to stop yourself.

II
Love Had a Thousand Shapes

Love had a thousand shapes...

was my mother's favorite line in all of Woolf.
Not that I expected her to be unhappy, but when I
walked into the nursing home she was laughing,
drinking coffee, books in bed, books stacked atop
the medicine shelf. *The thing itself before it has
been made anything,* shape of Lily Briscoe's wish,
that very jar on the nerves. My sense that things
were poorly rehearsed—the oyster-shell patio
was trying too hard, the Spanish moss ill-planned,
the clouds hanging from visible strings. Get that
and start afresh... I worried that her oxygen tubes
would get caught up, would pull a stack of books over.
I wanted to hold her. To fall asleep. When a storm
blew in I thought the building would turn over.
She was listening to *Madame Butterfly.*
Aluminum foil on the windows kept the room cool.

ii.

When I was a child my mother would stare, for what seemed like hours, out the kitchen window. She stared out the window and I stared at her, my silence mirroring her silence. Not until last year did I ask what she had been looking at: *Pears on the shed roof,* she said. *The clothesline,* her answer on another day. When I asked again she said, *I was worried your father wouldn't come home.* And after that—*You weren't old enough to understand.* One day she'd start: *We were still in love and your father was working.* The next she'd reconsider: *Everyone drank too much then.* After a while it didn't matter, the story had its own version apart from the one she chose to tell. A shovel propped against the steps. Smell of rotten plums. *I was always waiting for the worst,* she said. Wind through the screen door. A lemon-scented soap. Sound of our suitcases snapping shut, loaded with clothes and silverware.

iii.

Soon as the last bag of black beans,
the ultimate crate pocked tomato, the final meat, cold
or canned, had crowded the river
of the cashier's conveyer, my mother would create
the date, payee, amount, and her name,
always in that order.

Not a lie, but loop
and border more intricate than ivy, than a bee's wing,
the split nib maneuvering
with the ease of a gondola in which we might
have ferried home, had the town
flooded, had the roads

turned to water. *Jesus,*
get us out of here went my mantra, the near
women fanning with coupon papers,
children kicking the wire buggies, air getting raw
between them and *that woman up there*
signing the declaration.

The letter as lyre? A line
to appease the gods of green? A way for funds to be
insufficient interestingly? What-
ever propelled her pen reached apotheosis in
that moment past the quick ink-
drying breath, rip

and release to the cashier's hand,
a metaphysical drum-roll then impatience tilting
toward awe, a shopper or two
edging in, craning to see as through a lens
of at least a few possibilities—
Perhaps she could do

the wedding cards, and if
there were an autumn ball... but there was no ball
in Leakesville, and weddings were all
word of mouth, and despite a script that clearly
called for carriage, dress, and violins,
we walked—bags

in tow—through a town
that seemed, as ever, unwritten in, the same crop-
dusting airplane banking in and out
of view each time she stopped and looked up
as if it too might disappear inside
the black cash bin.

iv.

We broached it speculatively, the "afterlife," both
of us long since at sea, quotation marks like gulls
squawking in the airy hereafters of our propositions.
In her favorite version it will be an island,

boats freshly painted and lined bottom up
like unshelled peas all down the beach, none of the living
too eager to visit, none of the dead too eager to leave
their tropical soirée—Mel Torme high-balling

with an elderly Keats, Yeats moving in on Virginia Woolf,
Woolf moving in on time, our earthly suppositions
resolved like beaded bubbles winking at the brim.
But when she called, frantic, nearly weeping (she

had seen it—too dark, too cold, too nothing there
to gain one's bearings, voices, yes, but impossible
to hear except for the most meaningless of traces...)
I had to clear my head—*Calm down, Mom, you had*

a little nightmare about our old Zenith—and soon
she was laughing, telling what the doctor said, or some
story she'd read about Laurie Lee or Eric Blair
as if they, too, were boarding there, not off in that

sudden dank nowhere that we bridged again
by the thinnest of threads, holding balance, not
looking down *(stars, wind, low sounds*
by the shore), keeping our hopes to ourselves.

v.

My mother calls to talk about what a terrible mother she's been, how she drank too much, and after the divorce her awful taste for unemployed men, and never enough food in the house, though cigarettes filled every drawer. This is my cue to remind her that she hand-sewed all our costumes for the school plays. Saved for two years to buy our piano. Marched up to school every time I was suspended. And no matter whom I cussed or fought, she defended me. I go on like this with all the fervor of a Baptist preacher in the point-counterpoint that she and I embark upon so often in these last nights. Telling the story, measuring her life, though we never say it, in preparation for the eulogy.

vi.

I kiss her on the forehead, put my arm around her,
lock my fingers in her fingers, tell her I am sorry
as if she can hear me, as if she is still breathing.
I stand there waiting for her eyes to open, for her
hand to reach up and unsnap the old compact mirror
and, happy with her makeup, to rise from the bed
and walk out with me away from the doctors, the illness,
the dying. I pace around her body, as if she might
feel sorry for me and turn from the storied brightness
the newly dead are called into. I want her to feel
guilty, to give up the light and the tunnel or whatever
there is and come back for me, to put her hand
on my head and smooth my hair and call me baby.
But it isn't working. She isn't moving. I take off
my glasses and throw them at the wall then step
down until the lenses crack and the frames
are flattened so that she might know I am losing
my patience, my temper, and that I, too,
can wear out the nurses. And then the nurses
come for me, lead me out of the room. I do not
want to leave her body, flesh that made me, flesh
that feels no guilt, needs no protection, and offers
no comfort to me. I do not want to cry, do not want
to upset her. I'm sorry, I say. I'm sorry. I'm sorry.

vii.

My mother swatting a mosquito off my shoulder.
Sugar-sludge in the tupperware emptied of tea.
A pecan tree dotted with woodpecker holes.
To look at us from this distance it's hard to say

what we were thinking. I can't recall, but likely
it had nothing to do with the cement porch steps
cool on the back of my legs, or with the umber
light across the chinaberry and driveway gravel,

the sort of detail love looks for when calculating
what is real, what is supposition, and what
a wish for any condition under which the facts
might change. And she'd be here again, talking,

pushing up her glasses. To look at us from this
distance you might say we were happy then.
Grass growing over the sidewalk's edges. Slight
breeze. Lights coming on in the pastel houses.

viii.

When I return from the hospital the telephone is waiting, the calls have to be made. I go down the list of close relatives. "It's my mother," I begin. "She died tonight," or "she passed away." And when I hear the crying erupt on the other end I listen as a demigod might listen to the tears of mortals. Each voice seems that far away, and I have to not feel the news that I deliver, or else how begin, "her heart stopped," or "she was sleeping"? I have to speak, even if my voice is the voice of shock, of death announced, of a necessary delusion expired, the end of the lie we all tell one another each time we touch before departing: I'll see you again. The world will stay the same.

ix.

Far to the left of the placard that read ETERNAL URNS,
a cardboard container. To the right, a vase worthy
of Liberace's bedside table. My sister named a mid-
range gang of three, "Last Thermos," "Quaker Oats,"
and (her favorite) "Prince Edward in a Can." I think
we freaked the clerk out with our "silly mourners"
routine, which seemed, I would guess, odd, disrespectful.

Or perhaps we were nothing special, not the first
customers ready to be hustled amid the airtight
silver-plated resting places. Not so unique in our relief
that a few jokes left us feeling sophisticated, less
transparent, almost in control, our faces still swollen
from the doctor saying *She's gone, Mr. Kimbrell,*
we couldn't get her back—like stepping into

another country, the sea off-kilter, the sky tilted, the city
in the window exiled, muted, and I was thinking
She can see us. There was no other way to believe it.
A nurse led us into a room that didn't seem
anywhere. My mother's jewelry in a white envelope.
Then someone's hand on my shoulder. A man
we did not know kept telling us what time it was.

x.

My mother and her friends by the apartment pool
(bouquet of chlorine and piña coladas, coconut oil
and B&H 100's) that Saturday before we left the city,
and left Miss Billy, and Eula, and Barbara Yancy.

Ceramics, Carol Burnett, and knitting kits were in
(Miss Eula, Lord save us, had fashioned her own
elastic-free bikini). After that, we'd not see them.
Missed friends. Unpaid bills from old addresses

that smelled like ink and mothballs in their labeled
shoe boxes. Crickets and pine straw in the pool filter.
The sound of applause after my last back flip, jack-
knife or cannonball. So long, Miss Billy, and Eula,

and Barbara Yancy. I tried all week to find you.
If you should ever read this, my mother wrote out
a few requests: "Do not pay these credit cards.
Please call these people when I'm gone..."

xi.

My sense that things were poorly rehearsed: guests
came early. Flowers came late. The music was
not my mother's Maria Calais or Leontine Price
or even Midori's Paganini, but "Amazing Grace"
through a muzak loop that set my sister on edge.
The microphone buzzed at first, then the eternal
habitations, we beseech thee, then a reading
that I tried to follow, everyone in pews behind me.

I worried someone would skip a step on the way up,
that a candle would burn the sleeve of a robe,
that our old priest would ease out toward us
and reaching for balance, would lean his dangerously
antique weight in the wrong direction, turning
an ankle, or a hip, and then what? The floor
sinking into the ground, the whole building gone
trapdoor, light on the walls starting to crumble.

What guilt did I inherit that let me think everyone
(but the doctors said she'd been doing better)
secretly felt I was to blame? I said I was sorry.
I took her medical records to the best attorney.
I kept thinking that night of Faulkner's Addie Bundren.
The plank coffin. The cramped body. The town
staring down that poor load: the dead and the lame.
The foaming, impossible river of shame.

xii.

Everywhere I went my mother went with me:
though she was dead, she stood beside me
as I hacked away at the tea olive, blotching
the green patio. She looked down upon me
when I told my wife that I couldn't handle
the day of what words we had left, go ahead,
get out, I brought some boxes. When I
turned my house into the cave of drinkers
my mother drank too, but with disappointment.
She kept checking the shelves, convinced
that someone had walked off with a book.
She called the cops. She slipped
them money when they took my license.
"Are you for me, or against me?" I shouted
at her, but how could she answer? I walked
down the road beneath the power-lines
and the three fat crows and when I came
to the end, to the stagnant ditch water
and the hubcap and the beer can, my cup
did not runneth over, nor did my mother
fill it for me. What did I expect? I laid
down by the fence post in the gravel
and the garbage and the weeds and the road kill
until the buzzards circled over me
like painted birds above an infant's crib.

xiii.

After the dream I pull the ottoman up to my chair. Nothing but air where she had been sitting moments before—the first potluck I had hosted, and in her honor. All the guests were dead and busily disproving my assumptions about them: a man and a woman talking in the corner, someone's daughter milling about by the table, dipping her celery into a small bowl. Though the light around them seemed gauzy, and though they moved about with a gossamer grace typically reserved for fashion models or the very rich, my mother's guests otherwise resembled the living. A man made a joke about the lampshade. Another held a cracker like a tiny nimbus above his head. Mom, I said, Kierkegaard distinguishes between the ethical, the aesthetic, and the religious, respectively, thereby placing art beneath—but before I could finish she leaned forward: *Lighten up, son.*

xiv.

More than twice the amount that her check could pay.
How six o'clock in the afternoon lit up the yellow
cut-off notice hanging from the doorknob. No power.
Light wind. A season of calm weather. My mother

at the end of the street, walking home from work.
I thought I'd clean up the carport (bucket of dirt,
busted weight bench, empty plastic flowerpots).
She's looking up, waving to me. I thought I'd drop

the notice on the ground (how six o'clock in the afternoon
lit up the yellow neighbor cat staring at my broom).
What my mother sees is the notice falling down,
my dustpan, hanging baskets dripping on the swept

concrete. (Her purse in one hand, book in the other.)
She's smiling at me, walking past the pine trees
at the edge of our yard. My mother is home. Light
wind. I can hear the charms on her bracelet jingle.

xv.

There is the shape of sound: someone passing
in a blue pickup. And the shape of light when the road
is all dust and the truck disappears. Shape of this sense
that the light isn't real, that the branches are not,

and the fence posts. This whole hill is the shape of years.
There's the shape of the dream in which she is with me
packing for her grave: postage stamps from Russia and Morocco.
A long tangle of costume pearls. A silk scarf. A telephone.

And the shape of this sentence intended to mean
that everything is all right down here (how uncommon
the light when clouds clear) in case she hears me.
There is the shape of love, which is larger than the shape

of loss, and of flowers I bring when I visit her grave,
and of the empty vases that I will keep with others
in the yard behind my shed: shape of a museum.
A florist's dump. A potter's field. And there is the shape

of the moss-colored sky, which is the shape of listening.
She is listening... shape of a wish when all thinking
is wishful, and all wishes known—Mother—(how elegant
the ivy... the sound of the creek is sweet and near).

III

Depression in May

shows up like a mailman unsure of his route, every day
but at a different hour, and always with a color advertisement
from the mall of good reasons, as when word arrives
that a schoolmate, William R., has passed, and you remember
a moment of his kindness, then realize, no not him,
that wasn't his name, but the one you had always
confused him with, until what holds is flat gray loss: someone
(who was it?) has died, and the hedges have grown
past the height of the window, and the night is a mélange
of unwashed dishes, stale laundry, the corrugated
covers of magazines across the bathroom floor, and every chair,
every un-fluffed pillow has been tested for its dose of relief,
every channel for its segment of mindlessness,
and you can bear it no longer, you finally walk out,
it doesn't matter where, away from that house
because you cannot shake it, cannot stop this relentless
searching of memory for a face that might match
this William that left the earth, that joined the choir of the invisible,
until what you find is yourself in the yard of a neighbor
you never bothered to meet, but there you are,
standing in the porch light as if to deliver
a long-awaited package, and you can hear your own breathing,
can hear the night parting as you lift your hand,
ready to knock, ready to speak, not
knowing what you will say when he answers the door.

Praise for the Ford LTD

When I walk out of the store with my cigar and BEE LUCKY
scratch-off card, I think I see our old LTD idling in its nest
of smoke, the car my father bought from one-armed Bernie Trotter
for three hundred bucks, the one with the muffler that swung like
an elephant trunk and failed to leave a trail of sparks only because
of the coat hanger my father rigged to hold it up. I want to ask
the man behind the wheel if maybe this isn't the exact LTD
that my sister turned from umber soot to golden tan with a water hose
and dish soap, the same seats that I rubbed down with baby oil,
though the seats before me are covered in what looks like
the cured hide of an exceptionally large Dalmatian, which I
hate to see, because if this is the same two-tone, two-door, vinyl top
LTD, then it is the one in which my father backed over our dog
who that day wore a green dog-sweater and got placed with her sweater
in the trunk and made an awful thudding rolling forward
then back when the car started and stopped until my father
pulled over at a dumpster and unloaded her, and was embarrassed
for us to see him crying. Not the story I'd tell a stranger
without buying him a beer first. And this guy would likely
get pissed off if he knew that his car had been wrecked,
that my father stomped out of the house one night and returned
in three days with the front bumper missing and the back
boasting a sticker that read "Tyson's Beer Garden." That car
with its teeth knocked out. My father slept in the back seat
for a week after that, empty cans of potted meat and cracker

wrappers junking up the dash. Still, I want to say to this man
"Excuse me sir, we had this car when I was a kid," but I don't
because he might take it wrong, like I was saying "damn
that car sure is old," and it had been more than twenty years
since my parents decided to stay together and drove
along the canopied roads outside of town until they had
to scream at each other. My mother traded that car
for one day's use of a moving truck, and I didn't miss
my father much at first, but I missed that car, and bolted
baskets to my ten-speed, which it must have seemed
I didn't quite know how to ride, wobbling home with the weight
of canned beans, Tab, toilet paper, and milk. "Nice ride,"
I say to the man before he pulls off. "I'll sell it to you,"
he says, and revs the engine, lets off the gas, and the car
goes dead. But I don't care, for in this moment, I do
want to buy it, if for no other reason than to ride once again
with the radio stuck on A.M. *W God is Lord in Mississippi!*
To say amen to the viscous stench of scorched oil, to the slack
brakes and the stuck horn and the shot rod. Amen to the people
looking down at us from the windows of the city bus
while the upholstery above our heads flapped like a flag
in a hurricane of spilt beer, Little Debbies, and the combustible
fumes of hot tamales. "How much?" I say to the man, but he's
not paying attention because the car won't crank. He gets out
and lets loose with "Son of a Bitch! Son of a Bitch!" and I
think of telling the man that the car's only flooded, that if
he waits a minute it'll start, but he's too wound up,
"It's yours!" he says. "Try it again," I say, and he does,
and it starts, and he backs out of the parking lot, and I stand there

waving like I just got the better end of that deal, which is how

Bernie Trotter must have felt with his cigar hanging out

of his mouth and him waving us off with his one good arm

after my father had kicked the tires and honked the horn,

and my mother sat in the middle close to him, and even my sister

seemed happy when she punched me in the leg and called me

a dumbass, and we both laughed our guts sore with our hair

blowing and our hands held out, cupping the new wind.

Wings

As Moses first parted the bulrushes as preamble to the Red Sea,
  so too did I part my hair after that first rosy-fingered dawn
    when my sister performed the trick of feathers on my bowl cut,
      and the yellow school bus rubbed its wheel against the curb
        as if to say, Jimbo, you a fox! I was not a fox. Nor was I a bird,
          but those were the days when the fried-sugar scent of Aqua Net
            filled the Jr. High bathroom, and everyone wore their hair
              brushed-back, shellacked in a windblown manner that, sprayed
            into place, defeated all wind and was not to be touched
            anymore than you would touch the feathers of the bluejay,
          or the angel, or the chicken unplucked. Now, when I peek
           into the uniform abyss of yearbooks, and witness that hard
            hair of flight, that part straight down the middle as if rendered
             in an ecstasy of high-speed levitation, I remember how we
             grew to believe that every age had been an age of wings,

             or wigs in the style of wings. Icarus a kid we would have
            hung out with had it not been for the failure of his wings.
          Mona Lisa a classic but wingless beauty until my friend,
         Big Ed, anointed her head with his ball point bic. But just
       as Moses rose up and said, "free my people!" and they hiked up
     their dusty hems and crowded through until the sea collapsed
   behind them, so too did we give up our feathers for the fresh
freedom of the slick pull-back, the spiked middle, the myriad
variations on the military look, and stood on that first day

of our new cut, amazed at how much smarter we appeared,

how ready to be delivered by this latest of styles, though

we knew not where. O backward glance! O bad hair

of yesteryear! O vanity beneath a sky clear as a Windexed

mirror! That's better, I said, one sunny morning, and brushed

the past off my chest, and left my wings in the barber's chair.

Bahia Grass

For any kid who plucked it, who let its forked
bud and skinny stem dangle between the teeth,
who let its juice spike the mouth, for any kid
who took it out just long enough to hock and spit,
it lent a look of hard-ass wisdom, of farm-town
brazenness, a look that said *I drove that truck*
with one hand and unsnapped your sister's bra
with the other. And that was the look
that we were after.

                We? How comfortably
I fall back on the royal voice, old myth of the pack
just thinking of it, sour chaw of adolescence,
slim green camouflage for the four-eyed, zit-
plagued, cracked-voice wuss of a self that I
was ever busy ditching. I would have chewed
a pine tree to look a little tougher. Instead
I chewed that plain weed even as I hated it,
even as I mowed and baled it, straddled
rafters and stacked it high in the dust-choked,
wasp-choked air.

           Always there, common as dirt.
It's black gnat-sized seeds stuck to my shoes
on the way to school. I didn't care so long
as I could pick it, go sit on the steps and spit
with the others, and mull over which field

the deer were in, about which I'd learned little,
or discuss the full, round mystery of breasts, about
which I'd learned even less, though I talked
with the authority of he who knew, of he
who spoke with a kind of grass in his mouth.

To Keats in October

There they are, a few dusk-drunk swallows
    up at five o'clock from their eaves and awnings.
      See, these born-again impresarios
of smokestack and steeple still dip and swing,
and we, if we watch their upgathering, still
    disappear into the veil of things just
      out of eyeshot. Is it too naïve, too simple
to think if they're here, then you, too, must
be on wing above the buildings and traffic,
    dryad of light-poles and trees? What a view—
      and how not to swoon in this arithmetic
of flaring branches, this sensorium
    of twitterings? How not to believe that you
peer now—don't you?—down through
      the leaves—the claret-colored roof of autumn?

The Gulf

—for my mother

On the fourth birthday of your afterlife
I rent a house that might as well be in
the ocean. Two circumspect pelicans
drift across my watery yard. And if
I get a yen for fish, I can cast my line
right off the front deck. And look! There's a skiff
piloted by Señor Hemingway himself.

But that's not true. This is not an island
of ghosts. I don't even think that there's
a graveyard near. There's a little road,
and a tackle shop, and a general store,
and then the gulf, which I can almost see from here...

Which is to say that I miss those grand
versions of any circumstance that you
found too minor, too cheerless or bland
to report sans fiction, choice residue
of a blatant lie, your one-woman band
marching in some exaggerated aspect of a negligible truth.

Therefore, the sand is not off-brown, it's white
as Siberian snow. The stretch between it
and this house is not a fetid swamp but
a "mosquito preserve." And this is no

ersatz island lullaby composed of woe,

but a testament to you whereby

a few clouds drift across a cloudless sky.

Up Late, Reading Whitman

whose soul was like a spider, but was also like the grass,
and the meteor, and the beach at night, and I
would be honored if my soul was like the neighbor's dog
who tunneled beneath his fence today, black-eyed,
wagging, unclipped toenails clicking on the sidewalk,
all thick tail and barrel chest and neck fat, searching
the hedges for the scent of foe, the site of relief,
for a long-lost loping collie he might have known once
when the day was all sun, and the eternal tennis ball
barely touched the high grass, and the squirrels
couldn't help but admire his splendor,
for happily did he slobber on the sneaker and the hand!

My sister who is a young girl again
brings Walt Whitman to the party in the back of the house.

She is so proud. She has kidnapped
the poet and brought him to me—he keeps snapping his fingers,

he still believes he's at the docks.
He walks to the mantel and picks up a trumpet and turns to me

"You know the song of the soul?" he asks.
"Right," I say, and we step out to the porch where my parents

are sitting in lawn chairs,
and I play perfectly the first four notes of "La Vie en Rose,"

but no one is dancing. "Here give it to me,"
he says. "I fear you are hitting the notes of dream—your eyes

have been the same as closed
most of the time," and his cheeks puff out like old Satchmo's

and I'm happy as a bald-headed man
in a rainstorm of fedoras until the song is over and my parents

sit down and my sister runs up
and tugs on his beard. "But Walt," she says. "Your ride is here,"

and walks him out to the Brooklyn Ferry honking in the driveway.

———————

Walt Whitman, when I opened your book again this morning I thought
        I saw a page slip out from between "A Promise to California,"
        and "A Leaf for Hand in Hand," but it was just the robust love
        of my neglected utility bill.
And yet, the way it fell, first gliding, catching the light from the east

57

window, then end over end, it almost made me want to write
   a check for all that I have left unpaid.
Because a body has to pay the bills, and loves to walk to the store
   in winter and buy a newspaper and stamps for later
   and a coffee for now.
Because the soul is always looking around for its likeness in the limbs
   arching over the concrete, or in the specter of the yellow
   bicycle lying in the snow, or in the eyes of the woman
   at the register whose nametag says "Mary Shelley," though she
   does not know the other Mary Shelley, and certainly claims no
   relation, though what body is not a relation?
Which is to say, Walt Whitman, lover of loitering horses, stenographer
   to the stars, that when I write my check for two-hundred-
   and-some-odd dollars, and I lick the dry envelope, my tongue
   on the paper will make a sound not unlike a shoe pressing
   into snow.
A body and a soul.
Body licks the envelope.

      Soul walks quietly across the white field

----

and knocks on my door and hands me a pamphlet in which all
the letters are O's.

When I invite my soul in he runs his hand along the walls
to check for hidden mirrors.

He squints his eyes at me as if to tell my fortune: "Weren't you wearing that shirt eight years ago?"

When I ask my soul if he is the alpha or omega, dream or fact: "Here's five bucks," he says. "You need a damn haircut."

He sits down, and I bring the tea and biscuits, a remedy for amnesia. He talks about his life as the moon,

and as the dog for whom the moon is a bone in a distant stew. He says he does not worry

where he will live after my breath is a bogus address. When I ask what time his train departs,

he says, "The caboose's future is the engine's past."

———————

To speak of the soul is to invite criticism:
    Dear Criticism, your company is requested
at the home of Walt Whitman, kosmic bamboozler,
    revisionist of the grass; you, your lover,
        or husband, or wife, are warmly welcome;
    mechanics, southerners, new arrivals, your cousins,
        your complaints, fears, early memories, your lizards,
            your potbellied pigs, swearing parakeets,

that gorilla that speaks sign language (KoKo?)
your drunk friends, your grudges, your bad checks,
your motel matchbooks, your anima and animus,
your spirit coyote, your dream logic and sepia-
tinted photographs, all, all are welcome!

———————

I walk over to help my octogenarian neighbor fill the hole
beneath the fence where his dog dug out; he hands me
a shovel and says "I'll get a wood fence next spring,"
and adds, without a shred of self pity, "if I'm around
that long." Then he shapes his mouth into an O
and widens his eyes and holds his hands up in his best
impersonation of a ghost, a glad ghost, a laughing ghost
with his labrador running around him in circles,
an old man living in the knowledge of his death,
of the hour approaching when he will leave his house,
and leave his workshop with its wall of ham radios,
and leave all the antennas sprouting like corn
along the edge of his roof, and the frequencies that pull
a million voices through the air.
                          How not to think of you there,
Walt Whitman, spokesmodel for the universe, pamphleteer
of the snowflake and the cloud and the uncombed hair,
all of it an instance of soul—my neighbor and his dog
and the middle of the day and the gravel we shovel

before adding the dirt, and the dirt we tamp down lightly,
and the grass we put on top of that, grass that you loved,
exhibit "A" in the case for life everlasting, great-great-
grandchild of grass from ages ago, grass which is
its own museum, which grows out of itself, then dies,
then grows again, in the ditch—the Lord's carpet,
by the railroad tracks—the loose cargo's landing strip,
in the cracks of the sidewalk, grass which is its own
sidewalk where the living and the dead step toward each other.

The Author

Wayne Denmark

JAMES KIMBRELL

was born in Jackson, Mississippi in 1967. He is the author of a volume of poems, *The Gatehouse Heaven* (Sarabande Books, 1998), and co-translator of *Three Poets of Modern Korea: Yi Sang, Hahm Dong-seon, and Choi Young-mi* (Sarabande Books, 2002). He has been the recipient of a Ruth Lilly Fellowship, a "Discovery"/*The Nation* Award, *Poetry* magazine's Bess Hokin Award, a Whiting Writers' Award, and has received fellowships from the Ford Foundation and the National Endowment for the Arts. His work has been included in the *Bread Loaf Anthology of New American Poets* (University Press of New England, 2000), *American Poetry: The Next Generation* (Carnegie Mellon University Press, 2000), and *Legitimate Dangers: American Poets of the New Century* (Sarabande Books, 2006). He is a graduate of Millsaps College, the University of Southern Mississippi, the University of Virginia, and the University of Missouri-Columbia. He lives in Tallahassee with his wife, Jennifer Westfield, and is currently the director of the creative writing program at Florida State University.